MW01222413

On Following

By Meg Ziprick-Rieder

Copyright © 2016 Meg Ziprick-Rieder

All rights reserved.

ISBN-13: 978-1539002550

ISBN-10: 1539002551

"...yet he knew how to make madness beautiful,

and cast o'er erring deeds and thoughts

a heavenly hue

of words..."

– Lord Byron

"There's a blaze of light in every word

it doesn't matter which you heard

the holy or the broken Hallelujah"

– Leonard Cohen

Benjamin, Talia, Otto, and Jubilee:

I have not been the most stellar mother at making

scrapbooks, picture albums, memory chests...

However, I hope the words that I have tucked in tightly all

around you will bring you warmth, courage and joy

on your journey.

Contents

Horseshoe Lake, Jasper: An Autobiographical Poem

I jumped in Horseshoe Lake

from such a reckless height

it was a sacrifice

Instinctively I knew

I would be re-baptized,

emerge wholly new

from the frigid water

But your baptism was too slippery

it fled from me too easily

I could not keep it

or capture fallen drops

So I surfaced, solitary

still unchanged

on the stony shore

In recent years have I remembered

how our first ancestors

clawed onto these same primordial shores

air piercing aquatic lungs

It took millions of years

for them to shed their stiff, reptilian skin

to pulse warm blood

through waiting veins

Magi

Sometimes I wonder

if the immense madness of Byron and Wilde –

perhaps of every poet –

could be summarized

it would be this:

they could not find you

And I am afraid

that I too am fated

to be forever a Magi

following, following

star-searching

dread-filled, cold

arid wandering

And I am afraid

because if the poets could not find you

how will I?

Still, this swaying hope whispers

there are worse ways to waste one's life

than searching for the divine

Poem

Too long have you remained captive in my mind

imprisoned, frozen

long, sinewed arms reaching

beauty unknown

And I suspect that –

just like all the men (pre-Paul)

that I dated and discarded –

I have been terrified

to commit to you

And of all the shame I carry

perhaps you, poem,

have been my worst betrayal

Here now you are re-born

slowly and viscous

to morph as you will

(you were never mine to own,

you were never mine to fear)

I have heard a rumor

that a fluttered verse

can heal the world

I send you my breath

Berg Lake, British Columbia

Dusk-long have we heard

the glacier calve your words

broken, poured

broken, poured

Your substratum voice

flowing, winding still

through these caverns of time

And I wonder

is this the communion you wanted

that you asked us for

so long ago?

As I watch the ice fall into the waiting, lifting expanse

– it is love –

and I think, maybe, even I could do this

Glacier-bread, water-wine,

tender, reverberating still

Do this…

be broken for me…

be poured out for me…

be broken for me

Ptarmigan Trail, Kananaskis (Confession)

Most of my life I have felt mute

with such an appalling gulf

between what I intend/imagine

and actually say

These stiff lips seemed shackles

baffling, cruel for one who craved eloquence

above all

Even pen and piano

felt faulty instruments

to atone for such a deficit

And at just the moment

when I most desired

to be an unfiltered mouthpiece

voicing your clear, complete words

I was Moses, descending from the burning bush

unable to even utter of

your encounter

Yet here, in this mountain meadow

where water is wrung from rock

I hear your whispered voice

It is gently weighted

quiet, not silent

It rustles alpine grasses

echoes buoyant in the breeze

It was here I wept,

planting that pain

It was here I first began to love

the quiet we were creating

together

Hymn

Winter's sharp beauty found me

moon brittle around me

taut breath, nearly freezing through

cold's crystalline rhyming

light's receding timing

I'll forget every secret but you

Spring's thaw gently falling

receptive, soaked calling

each blade shares its story anew

fringed leaves come asunder

hope tilted in wonder

I'll forget every secret but you

The summer sun saved me

heat's memory fading

my sadness, they stole it from you

bright petals colliding

life's fragrance abiding

I'll forget every secret but you

Autumn's funeral grieving

inhabitants leaving

they've whispered, the mystery's true

gold colors swirl flying

earth's symphony dying

I'll forget every secret but you

Easter (Jubilee)

She cried in disappointment

as she said we told her

you were going to become alive today

and she was believing you would, long-awaited

actually appear

And so I quickly, playfully explained to her

that you are a god who likes to hide

in unexpected places

and be found

So we made a game of all the places we could find you

and all day we have been searching for you

in the sky, in the willows

in the stars, in her heart

and she has been soothed and delighted by the idea

(But all day long I am trying to swallow the sharp shards

and bury the ache too deep for her to see

because I don't want her to know yet

how often I have longed to come to you

and searched –

and I tell myself, of course you were there –

but each place stayed tomb-empty

and I never did find you)

Consolation Lake, Banff

I was smitten from the start

each rock, shore, sky

so saturated,

permeated with you

that I cannot here imagine

how I have ever found you anything

but present

And all I know is your beauty has haunted me

from birth

Yet something in me

so badly wants it to be

tangible,

more

it betrays —

it is just beyond grasp

I cannot reach or catch

Though brimming full

it echoes hollow, a missing still

Like so many grainy fragments

all I can do is hold this earth

let it slip through unfurled fingers

and scatter it with love

For each grain is evidence –

it haunts me still –

even hidden,

it is enough

Advent

If you were a god we expected

we would have recognized you

Maybe you knew

coming as a baby

would disarm us

We would lay old wounds and weapons aside

to open-armed, finally embrace you

Maybe you knew a baby

would be the only way

we would ever hold god

carry you close to our breast

breathe you in and out

Maybe you knew a baby

would be the only god

we would be unafraid to love

Anna, Simeon (Luke 2:22-38)

Eighth day

cold stone

warm arms

Word life

soul pierced

flesh-god

The priests and praising

psalm marinating

you, whispering, present

Time

The rising and falling

cacophony, calling

and yearn for you, to

come

Lord, how can it be in this sacred scene

only two would recognize you?

How I'm haunted

I tremble

would have I?

Strathcona Wilderness Center (a.k.a. Retrospective Climax)

We sat there

the three of us

on that staggered bench

wild, frenzied wind

reflected in our eyes

Beside the lake that was once a lake

that is now but anxious grass

The children's laughter

dodging through the trees

dampening suffocating silence

Laughter that does not yet know

we are question-laden

We possess a ragged inheritance

culminating to this moment

Timid it is uttered here

hushed, protected from exposure

Do you think we could go to hell for not believing in hell?

We had no answer

Yet since that day

something so tightly gripped inside

has gradually let go

until I realized

I am no longer afraid

of what you/I might do to me

You brought breath to that wound those years ago

this is what I want our children to know

To Our Willows

There are days I think

you have been more parent to our children than we

you have seen them through lengthening shadows

each season turning its wheel

Your stooping arms encircling theirs

limbs sustaining long years

They have fallen to you and from you

chording movement and sound

infusing supple spines with strength

And, at times, I have even been jealous of your patience

but mostly I am just ever, ever

grateful

For it is you who will remain long after we leave

I ask that you carry them

even then

Church of Wild

When I first heard about

the vast space-time continuum

and big history

with dimensions colliding,

bending and stretching

repeating

atoms being called into and out of existence

it frightened me to my utmost

So infinitesimally small,

I did not know where

in such a gaping cosmos

I could find you

Somehow you led me

to follow it to its worst

So when I learned of erratic quantum entanglement,

lurking dark matter and energy,

probability-existing particles, antimatter annihilation,

parallel universes with infinite histories,

and the fluctuating flavors of nothingness

it all seemed so insanely ridiculous and bizarre

that I could only believe

it had to have come from a heart

of play and whimsy and wonder

Now I love your Church of Wild

And I will follow

unafraid of the expanse

for the marrow of the universe is love

and your unknown is dense with hope

in finding utter, astounding

awe

(De)evolution of Whale

What unnamed call beckoned you

after millions of years

terrestrial-tied

to leave this land

while safe, with still-pliant hips

taking borrowed lungs

to return to the violent expanse

floating farther to the tempest

till all hope of return was void

What faith-seed spurred you

flung you far from stable shores

Was it a timid trusting

or a desperate plunge to the fray

And from my land-locked perch I wonder

if you have ever regretted your choice:

the thrill to dance amidst the turbulence

daring it to find you

strong and free

And I grieve –

What makes me so trapped and terrified

to follow in your wake?

Response on King David's 59th Psalm

Here David wrote,

"Destroy my enemies in your anger, God, wipe them out

completely"

These ancient, heavy words haunt us still

for after four thousand years

do we still celebrate those rumbling, tumbling stones of

Jericho

and frantically question, was that your voice

and how such things come to be?

Can I hope, believe...?

That it was like when I was six years old

when I heard your voice so agonizingly clear

and as I slowly crept through the tangled carpet

you undoubtedly told me

to take my sister's lightbulb eraser

because I had lost mine

and she had written a sign on our door that said

Amy's Room

But now, I think those could not have been your voice

because my sister has never been my enemy

and you, you have never liked stones

So how can I now celebrate those rumbling, tumbling stones

of Jericho?

When the churning crowds pressed each

to take up a stone to pound, cast

crush a nameless woman

you – in a single act of blinding love

that has stretched these two thousand years –

instead, you stooped

and wrote in the sand, laying every stone

bare

So how can I now celebrate those rumbling, tumbling stones

of Jericho?

David sang to you, "Destroy my enemies, wipe them out

completely"

And now,

after thirty-seven years inviting me to write with you in sand

I shudder,

do I still ask the same?

Mars/Ares: God of War

Too long have we stared transfixed in your orbit

grown dim in your shadow

while you left us dull,

burnt in your wake

From Cain's first blow to Abel

we have been fascinated, unable to escape

your pull

Too long have you promised prosperity

ensnared us in a choking allegiance

till we became void and afraid

till even our poets were betrayed

till I, too, have been played

a fool

But now we know what the Greeks did not

that you have only ever been a myth

a dying deity whose fiery gravity

is gradually crumbling

to rust

So tonight we are sky-searching

shifting our gaze,

looking for kinder constellations

to guide us

Wedding Poem

I would have created you

and borrowed your precision

to form your frame

I would have arranged you

in forgiving patterns

amidst calling depths

overflowing genesis

I would watch as you sparkle, shine

amongst dissimilar trees

to name you mine

Understand you I would not

but I would call you so familiar

And I would have painted you

in the solidest shades

gentle strokes, liquid grace

this is the place

I would worship

Certainty forming from the fray

illuming you

made, I'd say

Stay

Wishing Under a Bridge Canoeing Bow River, Banff and Aunt Nancy's Paraphrase

Jubilee: I wish that I could be a shape-shifter

Ben: I wish that we could do this everyday

Otto: I wish that I was a bridge

Talia: I wish that everything was exactly as it is

Me: I wish each of us joy and peace every day

Paul: Ditto

Aunt Nancy's Paraphrase

Jubilee: May we shift to the shape that God needs us to be

Ben: May we repeat and improve upon the good we do

Otto: May we be the bridge between what is, and what can
be

Talia: May we see and cherish the beauty in each moment

Meg: May we be blessed with joy and peace, and pass it on

Paul: May we respect brevity for the virtue it is

Perspective

I once congratulated myself that I was born with an artist's

heart

a connoisseur, slave to sublimity

each encounter impacting me in a profound place

With new eyes did I see:

How often our children ask me to play

How part of me is relieved when the vased flowers die

to make more counter space

How I debated cutting down our majestic willows

because they – as we – are so messy after a storm

How I can so readily shield myself from global suffering

How I gave away Grandma's homemade quilt

because it did not fit our bed

(I grieve that to this day)

Now I humbly repent,

recognizing I have so much to learn

about cultivating

and cradling

that which is beautiful

Otto

There is a palindrome secret to life

The universe repeating

written deep in your every cell

as a heartbeat

a ballad's hum

And you –

with your warm

unedged wisdom

will want to know it all

And you will stalk truth

grapple with it, mercilessly

What I hope you will find

is life needs to breathe to be alive

and truth that is hard

can never grow

But if it does

you will grow too

if you are malleable to learn

and gentle to absorb it –

a lifetime of beauty

Surely Eliot thought your name

when he wrote,

"...the end of all our exploring

will be to arrive where we started

and know the place for the first time"

Largesse

How is it so many of my happiest memories are wet:

Racing down mountain streams with Matt and Amy

Infant pictures being baptized by my own father

Tumbling through the Hellespont with Paul

Early camping mornings with cool cups of Tang from Mom

Grammy and Papa's coast house, bare feet on the bayou

The drenching joy of childbirth

As a child splashing cold glacier water on my face – I think
even then I suspected
I was being baptized over,
and over, and over

And now these four sculpted vessels are before me

I can only pray and hope

that enough of this largesse is flowing through to them

to flood their pitchers

for their own lifetime

of wonder

My Fear

I knew I lived in fear

when I realized how

I hold the store receipt strategically when I walk out

so all can see it

lest anyone accuse me of stealing

All the while simultaneously

touching the same receipt as minutely as possible

lest its bisphenol chemicals

be overly absorbed by my anxious palms

Until I learned that, as with every living thing

you, Fear, also fear extinction

and my quest to eliminate you

only served to make you stronger

So now I am trying not to oppose you

but to give you space and breath

even to grow if you will

We are cohorts in a strange symbiosis

nudging forces to support

I will not hide, flee, or banish you

And perhaps I even need you

Perhaps no beauty can be born

except through trembling hands

So each time I forget our truce

and feel the stifling

I send you warmth, I send you love,

I send you love

Lost-God

Trapping your voice in my memory

rewind you till it hurts

I left you long ago

Were you love or fear

lost or found

man or god?

Questioning these lines flowing parallel in my gaze

Filtering the residue

chain-warped freedom

hope in you

the wisdom of a girl

Fatal flaws I find in me

(replay you slowly, I can see)

you so good, and I merely

a beech tree

Talia Grace

It is her sixth spin around the sun today

the first few brilliant turns now long past

since first holding her tiny celestial/terrestrial newness

Physical laws state the motion is constant

but I sense/dread/swear it is accelerating,

fear the spinning will grow manic, pulsar

and out of control will I be forced to release this grasp

She spins and I cannot keep up

Six years has she spun on this heliocentric sphere

but I have orbited her

Why does she so cherish the compliment of how she is

growing

(those same words that I hear subtly pierce)

And if God is the ultimate parent

how can God bear to let us grow?

So each moment with her today is holy –

finite moments always are

Sun shining on her, attempting

to capture each unique spectra she radiates

She remains transparent, still I know

days of translucence and opacity lie ahead

so I absorb the all-of-her she offers me now

I have held her within, held her in arms

now she is arm's reach

Still she keeps aiming higher, further

(how does she defy gravity so?)

Her gaze is atmospheric, she is made to soar

A cosmic ambivalence – to want her to reach all

be a universal gift,

yet wanting her close – I remain on ground

Her trajectory unscripted

to marvel in who she is becoming

If only one word could travel with her

it would be a prayer and whispered plea...grace

Let her intimately know grace

Words cannot contain the immense gratitude for these past

spins

a gift we cannot deserve or control, but wholly welcome

Happy birthday, beautiful, beloved girl

Fortress Lake, Jasper (Ben)

You stood tall by each pine

washed hidden in the rain

Your every footstep holy

through this corridor of giants

And here, I pray that your faith will remain

unafraid of flux

In such swells embracing

this church of wind and waves

Past the weary arguments:

birth and death,

now and then

A glorious mixture

of structure and shadow

Your heart is heavy, I know

but there is refuge here

and they will not harm you at the water's edge

You will rest by the lilting river

where form and flow both dwell

it's syncopated promise pulsing

it is well, it is well

it is well

Unmasking

We were to told unmask

so I unraveled a small scratched story

Too-narrow it became binding

as it belied, I stumbled and stuttered

unable to tell

of your sweeping generosity

If given the chance

to go back, mask handed whole

unburnt, I would claim it from the fire

speak of the wonder of

beauty from ashes,

transforming hope

Confess your whole-yet-fractured paradox

And when the time came to hesitate,

to surrender it to the flame

I would step softly from the circle

fold my mask gently,

place it gratefully in my pocket

to care for it

Zero

You have been specter from the start

viscid, stalking

through the passage of years

I know why the ancients abhorred you

you never could be tamed

your endless abyss infecting

where nothing escapes unscathed

And in a world so desperate to matter

your empty has been too vacant

to bear

In recent tides, now

science redeems you,

the artists befriend

though you baffle us still

And I, too, am trying to trust, that —

Not every hollow will hurt

Not every void

must be filled

Athabasca Pass, Jasper

Mere hours ago

we stood here night-silent

where Mars hung brightly

reflected rippling in the waves

And now I stand still

the mountain pass awash

in halo-promised sunrise

Deep calling to deep

you hold me here

I await

and you have not released me yet

But we have children and tents

and trails to conquer

I waver, yet retreat

We have life, so I leave

Each twisted step a tinged regret –

unknown, what you might have given

Squandered now will it stay

for even if I could retrace

each step since your encounter,

it's fleeting

The sunrise remains

but the moment has passed

Wounded

You made yourself vulnerable

when you formed us –

this cord between us,

too easily trampled

held hands, too freely forgotten

A poet, pursuing a love

that would flee from you

I want to treat you tenderly

sharing the soft places

where we are fragile

Perhaps the purpose

of the cross

was to prove to us, you could

be wounded

Gray

We took you, ill-fitting gray,

and hung you on our shoulders

You proved a heavy hiking companion

Your tendrils too often

would wrap and obscure

disorienting, once smooth steps

made lurching and labored

At first your presence

ached acute loss

Though once shouldered

we were able to stand, weighted,

unwelcome though it was

Now, accustomed to clouded years

rebalanced under your hue

there lingers only barbed bittersweet,

a reminder of once-was

And through these compromised travels

I would no longer choose to leave you

Your murky filter revealing depth –

withheld, reluctant beauty

And now, we hike these trails with children of our own

With wistful reverence

do I drape you gently

on their shoulders as well

Evolving

Perhaps evolution

is the most beautiful metaphor

we could find

It is shaped slowly

as a poem

A universe bearing

greater God-image

each passing turn

Every string tuning

into more soulful song

Your infinite exhale,

until there is nowhere

that does not hold you

And if the universe is expanding still

perhaps it is only

to have more space

to carry you

On Finding

I imagine it might be like this…

One dusky evening I will walk into our garden

pass the potatoes lightly, brushing through the maze

to the clinging peas and stretching dill –

the scent that always makes me ache for Grandma and

Grandpa

I know the soft, warm, familiar soil

that has always welcomed me

will welcome me again

And as I kneel

each leaf gently rustles

a thousand poems I have been longing to hear

Trembling breath when I realize

they are all, all of them

are love poems

Hands tender, holding that which was dross –

it's all treasure to me now

You are here

Your hands press mine

as we gently unfold each plant

marveling how they have grown

how they are alive

And all that time, I see it now,

was love

And I wouldn't even want to hold you to account

for it was all prodigal beauty,

and what a wondrous journey it was to follow, to find,

to be found

Acknowledgments

Paul: I was a pretty horrific Enneagram 4 when we met. Since then, my life has grown exponentially in contentment and joy because of you. I love doing life with you. Thank you.

Mom and Dad: You have woven faith and story into my life. Your examples of grace and forgiveness are examples I hope to aspire to. Thank you for the rich memories and inheritance you have given.

Mom and Dad Rieder: You have always welcomed and accepted me, and our eccentricity. I hope to emulate your support for us in our own children's lives. Thank you.

Amy, Leah, Claire, Matt: Writing requires so much vulnerability, which I couldn't risk if it weren't for your friendships. Thank you.

Talia, Jubilee, Otto, Ben: You are so much more than anything I could hope for. Thank you for all you teach me.

Aunt Nancy (Wedig): Thank you for your beautiful paraphrase. You read our hearts.

Kristine Buchholtz: Amazing editor. Thank you.

Brian Zahnd: Thank you for your book "A Farewell to Mars" which inspired the poem "Mars/Ares: God of War". Charles Seife: Thank you for your book "Zero: The Biography of a Dangerous Idea" which inspired the poem "Zero".

Loving God: I don't understand you, but I trust you to redeem all things. Thank you for giving beauty and life.

About the Cover: A picture taken of the cliffs at Horseshoe Lake in Jasper, Alberta, which inspired "An Autobiographical Poem". We have gathered our courage and jumped from them – more than once! Picture and cover design by Paul Rieder.

About the Author: Meg Ziprick-Rieder lives with her husband and four children on a regretfully messy acreage in Alberta, Canada. She enjoys homeschooling and learning with their ever-interesting children. Hobbies are gardening, writing, reading, yoga, and backpacking.

72181124R00042

Made in the USA
Lexington, KY
02 December 2017